Puerto Rican Spanish

Learning Puerto Rican Spanish
One Word at a Time

MIDDLE
COAST
PUBLISHING

Iowa City, Iowa

Puerto Rican Spanish
Learning Puerto Rican Spanish One Word at a Time
ISBN: 0-934523-62-2

Edited by Timothy P. Banse

Editor@Middle-Coast-Publishing.com

DEDICATION

This book is dedicated to all of the wonderful people of Puerto Rico and particularly my friend Lianna Sisinni and her family.

Dictionary
&
Phrases

A.

A calzón quitao - Literally, without pants on. Back in the day, the expression meant something said without prejudice or tact spoken in blunt, honest language.

A cien por chavo - Figuratievely a dime a dozen.

A fuego - Particularly cool. Related words: Fueguembel, fuegoski, a fueguillo.

A juyir crispin - To run away.

A lo fortuño - Reference to a governor who violently and ferociously fired tens of thousands of public officials and then put them to work in the coffee industry (fields). Implies hollowness.

A lo loco - Literally like crazy, done without much thought.

A mi plín - I just don't care—the colloquial equivalent of, no me importa, in other Spanish dialects.

A pues bien! - Ah, Ok!

A ver si el gas pela - See Ay que ver como bate el cobre.

Abochornao - Contraction of the participle abochornado: to have bochorno. It is derived from Latin Spanish vulturnus, a hot and humid east-wind. As slang, it means red-faced with shame. Abochornao is the contraction of abochornado, or someone embarrassed.

Abochornarse - To be red-faced, ashamed or embarrassed, to blush.

Abombao - Smelly. A very bad or putrid odor, rotten, spoiled food. A damp cloth or fabric that smells from sitting out.

Acángana - In your face!

Achaques - The aches and pain of growing old.

Acicalao - Good looking. Aicalao can be used interchangeably with gato and gata, including the verb: Acicalar.

Acho, or Chacho – An abbrevisation for muchacao, guy. Used as a conjunction to bridge between thoughts like "well" in Engllish. Acho and chacho can also mean: what's up?

Acho men, or Chacho men - Oh man! An expression of disappointment or of surprise.

Acho que fiebre - Hot or feverish, as in liking something so passionately you have to do it, or wear it, every day.

Adobao - Contraction of adobado, to be seasoned with spices.

Afrentao - Contraction of afrentado. An outrageously selfish person. A glutton. Someone who greedily wants it all.

Aguacatao - Someone who is waiting to see when, or if, a situation will improve. Someone whose actions are guarded and calculated, an insecure person. A bump on a log.

Agujita y su combo - Literally, little needle (phonograph) and her combo. Slang for playing records, or CDs, instead of a live band.

Ah, pues bien!- Literally, "Oh, well then."

Ahora - Now, right now. Ahorita in the rest of Latin America.

A galletazo limpio - To beat up badly with your bare hands, slapping someone on the face, with open hands, instead of a closed fist.

4

A lo anibal - Reference to a recent governor of Puerto Rico who was accused of tax evasion and government corruption. A discreet way to imply thievery.

A mi, plín - A mi - Literally, To me. As slang, I don't care. Equivalent to, No me importa.

Ajumao - Contraction of ajumado or, drunk. Someone drunk, besotted, who reeks of alcohol.

Al garete - A garete is a rudder. When masts broke offshore in heavy seas and strong winds, the helmsman would sweep with the garete to make headway. This nautical expression means 1. Adrift, without direction or purpose. 2. But more commonly means, A lo loco, or crazy. Many Puerto Ricans mistakenly believe this is a local slang and that it is a single word algarete. But truth be told, the garete appears in Spanish dictionaries with the same meaning as above.

Al revés de los cristianos - Literally, The reverse way to Christians. An Old Spanish expression dating back to the times of the Moorish kings. Refers to something that makes no sense.

Alcahuete - The Old Spanish-Arabic word *alqawwád,* the gossip runner at the office or town. The matchmaker in illicit romantic relations. Also means to be extremely servile. Someone who spoils someone else (grandchild) too much.

Alcapurria - Deviled crab or beef.

Amargao - Contraction of amargado, embittered. Someone constantly depressed or bitter.

Amarillitos - Literally, little yellow ones. Fried plantains.

Ámeraaa y to'?! - This exclamation is typically screeched at the end of a juicy tidbit of bochinche, or gossip. Oh, my gosh! I can't believe it!

Anda pa'l - An abbreviation of Anda pa'l sirete, or the bad word Anda pa'l carajo. Also it refers to someone stunned, or amazed, or scared.

Anda pa'l carajo - Exclaims, Get the hell out of here! The carajo is the tip of the ship's mainmast, the crow's nest. Its wild, pendulum-like motion makes it a very dangerous and uncomfortable post. As slang, Oh shit!

Anda pal sirete - Oh, shit.

Añoñar - To show affection to the point of spoiling someone. It mostly describes the affections from adults towards their children and grandchildren.

Anormales - My crew, my gang, or when someone calls his/her group the best ones, or the sick ones.

Aplatanado - Someone lacking passion for anything, derived from platano, plaintain. Apathetic.

Aplatanao - Contraction of aplatanado. During the Renaissance (1492–1650) in Puerto Rico, some lethargic souls neither worked or farmed. Instead, they lived in caves, gathering and eating wild plantains and other fruit. Essentially a loafer, someone without ambition.

Apretao - Crammed. Denotes tough situations, as in between a rock and a hard place.

Àque es la que? - An abbreviation of: Àque es la que hay?, Literally what is it that's happening?

Aquetero - A liar.

Arado - Literally, an arado is a ploughshare. As slang, it describes someone so dim-witted so as to be unfit to work behind a plough. An idiot or a dummy.

Arao - An idiot or a dummy.

Arranca en fa - Beat it! Get lost! Go to bed! As from a frustrated parent speaking to their child,. Derived from a music expression which means Start on F (the musical note or key).

Arrancado - Ripped out.

Arrancao - Contraction of arrancado. Literally ripped out, as in pants pockets pulled out to show there is no money in them. To be penniless.

Arrebatao - Contraction of arrebatado, a spiritual rapture. As slang, it implies the rapture of the High (drug reference, not heaven), intoxicated.

Arrempujate pa ca - Come this way. Get closer.

Arrollao - Contraction of arrollado. An arollo is a creek. So, literally, it means stranded at the creek bank. As slang, stranded or left hanging.

Atángana - An interjection similar to, In your face!.

Atorrante - Classical Spanish for a bum. A good for nothing loafer.

Averiguao - The contraction Averiguado. Nosey.

Ay bendito! - Contraction of ¡Bendito sea Dios! Literally, Oh Blessed One. Voiced to show frustration or exasperation when complaining about something. An exclamation of woe or pity. The phrase often stems from a deeply-held empathic sense towards what is being sensed (heard, seen, touched, et cetera).

B.

¡Bendito!- Contraction of ¡Bendito sea Dios! Blessed be God. Equates to the English, Good Lord! Voiced to show sympathy or compassion.

¡Bicho es!- A vulgar expression meaning My Dick!. Used as an interjection meaning, No way! Or Hell no!

¡Boa! - Literally, a serpent (Boa constrictor). Used to playfully mock someone who trips.

Baba- Literally, spittle. As slang, boring, meaningless talk.

Babilla - Bravery, machismo.

Babosada - Useless, stupid, or nonsense.

Bacalaitos - Codfish fritters.

Bacalao sin cabeza - Literally, a codfish without a head. As slang, a bastard child.

Baile, botella y baraja - Dance, Bottle, and Cards. Used to allude to seemingly innocuous, even beneficial, yet premeditated, plans intended to keep someone entertained (distracted) while others (usually, the government) go about their business of failing to fulfill their expected duties or obligations.

Bambalan - A lazy bum.

Baraja - To distract, to keep entertained, oblivious to what's going on around. Historians coined this wry phrase to describe the government of Miguel de la Torre (1822-1837).

Barrio - A ghetto person's neighborhood.

Batata - A lazy, non-productive employees. Usually in reference to government employees.

Batey - from the Taino word, meaning a yard in the country.

Batú - Sport.

Bellaco - A sly person. As slang, someone in heat or having sexual desires.

Bellaqueo - Somone on the make.

Bemba - Lips.

Bembé - Series of Afro-Cuban dances dedicated to the orishas. Also bemba or bembe, for lips, when used without diacritical stress.

Bendito - Spoken to show sympathy or sorrow towards someone. Ay Bendito used to show excitement.

Bicha - A drama queen, someone rude and obnoxious.

Bicho - Literally, a bug. As slang, a common vulgar term for the male sexual organ.

Bicho/Bicha - Literally, a bug in Spanish. In Puerto Rican slang, penis, cock, or a girl full of it who believes she's above everybody else. Mostly said to girls of high society.

Bichote/Bichota - The guy or girl in charge of a group, a head honcho, or a pimp.

Bicijangueo - A corillo or group of Urban bicycle riders riding bicis and hanging out.

Bildin - Building.

Bizcocho e' titi - Literally, auntie's cake. As slang, something very easy, as easy as pie.

Blanquito - Little white person, or whitey. Sometimes used to refer to someone from a higher social class, or at least their perceived class. It has nothing to do with race or the color of one's skin.

Blin Blin - Bling or jewelry.

Blunt - A cigar hollowed out and filled with marijuana.

Bobo - 1. Feeble-minded. 2. A baby pacifier.

Bochinche, Bochinchoso, Bochinchosa - Gossip, gossiper. Also, describe a heated verbal argument between two or more groups of people.

Bohío - Derived from the Taino language, meaning a hut, usually without the benefit of walls.

Bola hinchá - Bola means a ball. But in this slang term, it stands for testicles. Hinchá, short for hinchada means swollen. 1. To be upset/bothered. 2. Women also use this expression, only with bola meaning an ovary instead of a testicle.

Bomba - Bomba dance.

Bombito al pitcher - Fly ball to the pitcher. It implies something easy to accomplish, as a fly ball hit to the pitcher.

Boricua – A Puerto Rican. Before the Spanish arrived on the island, the indigenous Taíno called their island Borikén (also spelled Boriquén and Borinquen). derived from the island's original name, but let's face facts —it's just more interesting than puertorriqueño (Puerto Rican)

Boricua - Borrowed from the Taino language, meaning Puerto Rican.

Borinquen - Puerto Rican.

Bregar / Bregando - To deal with something without an actual affirmative commitment.

Bregaste cajita de pollo - Similar to Bregaste Chicky Starr, meaning to act in a cheap or wrong way. Cajita de pollo refers to Fried Chicken Express, a Kentucky Fried Chicken-like fast food franchise from the 80s which sold 99 cent meals in small cardboard boxes packed with three very low-quality chicken wings and soggy French fries.

Bregaste Chicky Starr - Chicky Starr is a famous Puerto Rican professional wrestler (antagonistic). Also, know that the word brega refers to a bullfighter's dealings with cape and bull. The phrase implies someone who plays dirty or a betrayal.

Brevaje - A medicinal drink.

Brillando la hebilla - Literally, Polishing the belt buckle. As slang, Dirty Dancing.

Broki - Slang for buddy. Derived from the popular English language, bro. Ki renders it diminutive, making the term more affectionate (broski).

Brutal - The best or worst of something. Cool, amazing, fantastic.

Bruto - A brute, dumb, idiot e.g. ¡Que bruto! What a brute, an idiot!'

Buena gente - Good people, a nice person.

Bugarrón - Gay

C.

Como la puerca de Juan Bobo (or John Ninny) - Originates from a popular, classic, Puerto Rican folktale. Juan Bobo, a dim-witted hillbilly, was told not to take his pig to a fiesta. So he resourcefully disguised the sow in woman's clothing and took it anyway. The sow, being true to its nature, wreaked havoc at the fiesta. This figure of speech refers to a woman who overdoes her makeup and accessories to the point of looking ridiculous.

Cuatro de Julio - Literal for Fourth of July used to refer to someone who thinks they are better than everyone else. Depending on the context, it is also used when something or
someone is outstanding, similar to how the word Bad can mean something cool. It's also derogatory, an insult.

Caballo - Literally to bathe the horse, an archaic term for having sex.

Cabezicoco - Hard-headed, bone-headed.

Cabrón/Cabrona - A ram, or male goat. As slang implies a cuckold, a person whose loved one is unfaithful, a bad situation or object.

Caco - A derogatory reference to small-time thugs and who are fans of Reggaeton music. Derived from the Greek god of treachery and thieves, Cacus. Can also imply someone mentally challenged or who tries to look and act like a gangsta.

Caco-mobil - A Japanese car driven by caco's: heavily-customized and decorated replete with a loud bass sound-system, loud muffler and chrome-rims.

Cacus - Someone mentally challenged.

Cafre - Old Spanish Arabic for kafir, or non-Muslim. Denotes a barbaric, uneducated, vulgar, bad-mannered person reveling in his own coarseness. Low class, tacky, or ghetto.

Cagar(se) - Literally to defecate, to screw up, or to blow it.

Cagar mas arriba del culo - Literally, Shitting above your asshole. Describes a person who is doing something out of their league.

Cágate en tu madre - Literally, (to) shit on your mother. Equates to F--- you!

Cállate la boca - Shut up!

Camina con los codos - Literally, walks on the elbows. As slang, it alludes to someone who won't let go of the money in their hands no matter how hard they're hit on the funny bone. In other words, a cheapskate.

Candela - Fire, flame, heat, passion.

Cangri - An important person who's in charge.

Cangriman - A corrupt, opportunistic liar or bully. From the word congressman.

Cantaso - A hard hit to someone or to oneself, such as may occur by accident. Similar to Guatapanazo.

Cantio de un gallo - The distance a rooster can be heard when crowing. As slang, near proximity. Equivalent to the American English expression: Within a stone's throw.

Canto - A piece of something. Refers to reproductive organs.

Capear - Literally, to weather the storm. As slang, to buy drugs.

Caquear - To steal.

Carajo - Literally, the tip of the main mast on sailing vessel. The Carajo, the crow's nest, was the worst place to be sent on an ancient ship.

Cariduro - Hard-headed, stubborn.

Cáscara - Literally, tree bark or the husk of a fruit. As slang, someone dumb.

Casqueta - Masturbating.

Catimba - Refers to giving or enduring a beating.

Cayo como yuca - Literally, Like a yuca. As slang, he has fallen deeply asleep.

Cemí - An indigenous idol.

Cerrao - A contraction of cerrado. As slang, someone dim-witted, who lacks common sense, or someone closed-minded.

Cerrero - Cerro means a hill. Literally, Cerrero means pertaining to hills. As slang, it refers to an animal that has strayed away from humans and taken to the hills. A wild horse.

Cerrucho - People montan un cerrucho (mount a cerrucho), when everyone is broke. Basically, Puerto Rico lingo for donating money to a particular cause, whatever the cause might be.

Chacho - Used as a conjunction to bridge thoughts. It derives from muchacho, which means guy, or more specifically, man. Acho and Chacho are both abbreviations of the same word.

Chacón - Reference to Iris Chacón, a voluptuous TV singer/dancer on a variety show in the 1970s-80s. As slang, it alludes to a voluptuous. callipigian butt and hips. This makes sense when you learn Iris Chacón liked to show off her derriere before it was fashionable to do so twerk.

Champion - A name brand. Tennis shoes, sneakers.

Chanchy - Essentially, a jerk. A scathing appellation often bestowed on young, non-English speaking Latino/Hispanic immigrants.

Chanclas - Literally, house slippers worn by women inside their homes.

Chancletas or chanclas - Sandals, flip-flops, et cetera.

Chancletero - A man or woman who only fathers daughters. Derived from chanclas, the ubiquitous house slipper shoes worn by women inside their homes, meaning people not working outside the home.

Changuería - Describes the behavior of a spoiled youngster who throws a hissy fit when his parents did not buy him a toy, give him candy, or when he does not get to do something he wanted to do, like go outside and play. A youngster with this behavior is said to have changuería.

Chapusería - Literally, something done haphazardly. A job or workpiece slopped together, completed just to get it done and not completed with any degree of professionalism or due care.

Chapusero - Someone who performs sloppy, sub-standard work.

Charlatán - A clown. Used to refer to someone acting foolish or disorderly. Someone not serious in their actions or dealings. Someone who cannot be depended upon or trusted.

Charro - The Old Castilian cowboys back in Salamanca, Zamora and León, as well as Mexican cowboy, with the only difference being their hat. Whack appearance, as in, Ese tipo es un charro; Hillbilly; out of style.

Chavito - Penny (One-cent coin). During the Renaissance, the coin was the doblón (in English' doubloon). A notched, thin, wide silver coin that could be bent into eight pizza-like slices. Piezas de a ocho, or ochavos equal a piece of eight.

Chavos - A contraction of Old Spanish, ochavo, one eighth, the famous pieces of eight. Denotes money. Note that in Mexico, Honduras and Nicaragua, the word means, a guy.

Cheche de la pelicula - The hero who swoops in to save the day. Cheche is the mispronunciation of the word Sheriff in western movies.

Chévere - Cool or great. Also chuchín.

Chicar - To make love, only in the vulgar sense.

Chichaito, - A Puerto Rican mixed drink of rum and anise (suggesting chicar) chisme, gossip.

Chichar - To have sex.

Chililín - Just a drop, a little bit. Notice there are two letter Ls in this word.

Chilin'- Derived from the English word 'chilling' meaning to be or to feel cool or relaxed. Notice there is only one letter L in this word

Chillo / Chilla - 1. In PR, can refer to the tasty red snapper fish (ouchinango, pargo), but also 2. A lover or mistress.

China - Tasty, orange, citrus fruit. In Puerto Rico, China may refer to the country in Asia, the color orange, or the tropical citrus fruit. Know that the word Naranja, used for oranges in most Spanish-speaking countries, only refers to the bitter orange in Puerto Rico. The slang term originates from a 19th century brand of oranges imported to Puerto Rico advertised as: Naranjas de la China/Oranges from China. 2. A Chinese woman.

Chinchorrear - To go bar hopping. To hang out at bars.

Chinchorro - In Puerto Rico, a small, unassuming bar everyone frequents.

Chingando - To fuck or to have dirty, nasty sex.

16

Chingar - To fuck, as in to have sex.

Chinita - The colour orange.

Chiringa – Kite. In other Spanish speaking countries a kite is called cometa/comet after the tail.

Chiripa - Odd job.

Chiripas - Odd jobs.

Chiripiar - To do odd jobs.

Chivo - Literally, a billy goat. As slang, a mistake made while house painting the walls or ceiling. When one finds a spot on the wall that was inadvertently left unpainted or missed a second coat, that spot is a chivo. You missed a spot, un chivo.

Chocha - Literally, the lupine seed. As slang, a vulgar word for the female genitalia.

Chola - Head.

Chota - Whistle-blower. Snitch.

Chulo - Literally a pimp. As slang, something really cool.

Chumbo - Flat-butted.

Churras - Severe, liquid diarrhea that leaves one debilitated.

Chustro – An old car.

Clavar - To have sex with someone.

¿Claque?-What's up?

Cochino/cochina - Literally a pig. As slang, an unkempt and/or dirty person.

Coco - Literally, a coconut. As slang, the noggin, the head.

Cocolo! - From 1500 to the 1950s, a cocolo was a black from the Lesser Antilles, or British West Indies. During the British Slave trade, slaves routinely fled to Puerto Rico where by law, they were freed, given refuge, and 3939 square meters of land. Escaped slaves brought their own music, so today cocolo means someone who listens to Salsa music, typically older Big-Band Salsa music.

Cocopelao - Literally, a peeled coconut. As slang, it means bald-headed.

Cocotazo - A hit on the head that leaves a bump, especially when done by someone's knuckles.

Coger pon - To catch a ride.

Coger sereno - Sereno means serene, but also the cold, damp, unhealthy night air, so it means to feel the cold of the night.

Cogerlo a pecho - Literally, To take in the chest. As slang, To take to heart. Used as advice when someone takes something too seriously or when someone has been easily offended.

Cogerlo suave - To take it easy.

Coja - Literally, to fuck.

Cojones - 1. A vulgar way of saying that you'll do something because you want to. 2. Also, balls, as in testicles.

Colgar - Literally, to hang. As slang, To fail, to flunk school.

Colgar las tenis - Refers to someone that has to die.

Colgarse - Literally, to get hanged. To fail or flunk a class (in school).

Colilla - A cigarette butt, a wedgie.

Collera o Coyera - Someone with bad intentions or limited intelligence. Dumbass, a good for nothing, shady character.

Come gofio - Gofio is roasted cornmeal. In the Spanish Canary islands, they eat it dry and sweet. It sticks to the palate rendering one unable to speak for some time. As slang the term refers to someone who's not doing a whole lot, taking it easy, killing time, and babbling nonsense while all the while.

Comiendome un cable - Translates to: Eating a cable. As slang, me estoy comiendo un cable, it expreses borddom: I'm bored.

Como la gatita de Dorita, si se lo sacan llora y si se lo meten grita - Literally, Like Dora's kitty. Describes someone who's never satisfied. Dammed if you do, dammed if you don't.

Come mierda - Literally, Eat shit. It is used when referring to a petulant know-it-all. A person who thinks or acts like he is all-knowing and/or all-deserving. Also someone of a higher social status who prefers not to slum with persons of lower status. Essentially, a snob or an arrogant person.

Comerte la mierda - Eating shit, wasting time.

Como amarrar los perros con longaniza - To do something stupid, it makes no sense, like tethering dogs with sausage links.

Como becerro mongo - Like a newborn calf,
 weak.

Como cabro de costa - Like a goat from the coastal region which incidentally, are notoriously horny.

Como coco - Literally, like coconut. Refers to something or someone strong, robust, or resistant.

Como el cabro de minga - Horny like a billy goat.

Como el culo de la olla - Literally like the cooking pot's bottom, black. Referring to black people.

Como el rabo de la cabra - Crazy, like a goats tail.

Como el Rosario de la Aurora - Used to describe a party that ends up with a fight.

Como la puerca de Juan Bobo- Juan Bobo, a folkloric character in Puerto Rico, called Juan the dummy. Not known for intelligence, Juan Bobo notoriously overdressed and over-accessorized his pet pig. As slang,a woman that overdoes makeup and accessories to the point of looking ridiculous.

Como las tetas del toro – Literally, like tits on a bull. In other words, quite useless.

Como pirata de parking - Used to describe a person with an affection for the same sex.

Complejar de alguien - To have a delusion of being like someone else by having adopted characteristics of that person.

Con las manos en la masa - Literally, With the hands on the dough. Caught in the act. With the hands in the cookie jar. To be caught in the act.

Conchetumadre - Motherfucker.

Confianzú - Contraction of Confianzudo. A person who is too forward, who comes on strong or who is overconfident. Somebody so bold so as to making people uncomfortable, or who doe and says things that might be considered disrespectful.

Con la boca es un mamey - Something appears easy but isn't. Easier said than done.

Coño - Literally, a woman's private parts. An exclamation uttered when a person accidentally hurts themselves. Stronger than ouch!

Contribuciones - Taxes

Contribuyente - Tax payer.

Copao - Used to call dibs on something you like even though you have no chance of owning it. As in, "I call dibs."

Coquí - 1. A very small frog that inhabits Puerto Rico's El Junque National forest. The fog is named for its distinctive mating call : Co-KEE, co-KEE 2. Slang term for a Puerto Rican.

Corazón de melón – Literally, a melon's heart, the sweetest part of the fruit. As slang, a term of endearment for someone with a big heart.

Corillo - The word Corro spelled with a double R means a crew, or a group of people, who share similar ideas and habits, who all hang together. Simply put, a posse. While when the word is alternatively spelled with only single R it means a small choir.

Corillo melaza - A group of close friends

Corneta - Translates to a horn, implies someone who is not the sharpest tool in the shed.

Correrle la máquina, or Seguirle la corriente - To keep a joke going at someone else's expense, follow someone's lead incredulously, or tell others to with the intention of laughing at them behind their back.

Corricorre - A runaround, running out.

Crica - Female genitalia, crotch.

Cuajito - Chitlins.

Cuando Colon baje el dedo - Literally, When Columbus puts his finger down. A reference to the statue of Christopher Columbus in Plaza Colon in Old San Juan that presents Christopher Columbus pointing towards the heavens. This slang expression signifies that some particular thing will never come to pass. But in actuality, the expression is, Cuando Ponce de León baje el dedo, a reference to the statue of Ponce de León in front of the old Church of San José. Truth be told, the statue of Christopher Columbus at Plaza de Colón is not pointing at anything!

Cuernú - Derived from the word cuernos (horns), a symbol for infidelity. Should someone call you, cuernú, they're saying that you have horns. Therefore your partner is cheating on you.

Culan - Literally, engine coolant. As slang, the word refers to the female derrière due to its similarity with the synonymous culo. Popularized by entertainer Iris Chacon in a car commercial for Amalie Coolant.

Culebra - Literally snake, but can also mean penis.

Culeca o Culeco - Slang misspelling of clueca or cluec, broody as in broody hen. A happy person who is excited with a victory or good news long-awaited.

Culeo/Culear - Mean-dancing, dirty Reggaeton, or shaking the booty.

Culiando - To shake one's ass, twerking.

Culito - Little ass/butt.

Culo - Meaning ass. Can also be said as a contraction, as cu' (culo).

D.

Dale percha (pronounced pelcha) - Literally, to put it on a hanger. As slang, it means to take it off or don't wear it anymore.

Dame un sippi - A small try or a sip.

Dar chinas por botellas - Literally, to exchange oranges for bottles. Back in the day, when returnable bottles were still in use, some merchants exchanged oranges for empty bottles. These days, as slang, it denotes an unfair trade or exchange. Comparing apples to oranges.

Dar culo - Literally, to give one's ass. As slang, it means to not give one's best performance or to give up altogether.

Dar pa'bajo - 1. To kill someone. 2. To have sex with a woman.

Dar un tumbe -To steal something.

De cualquier malla sale un ratón - Literally, from any net a mouse might come running out. Implies, don't be surprised if this happens.

¡Deja el tripeo! - Literally translating as stop tripping! It means enough with being a party-pooper or focusing on the worst-case scenario.

¡Dejó los tennis en el piso! - He sprinted so rapidly that his feet came out of his shoes!

De Malla/mallita - To be all net.

De rola or Irse de rolimpin - Keep moving, go somewhere else.

Dembow - The rhythm used to describe reggaeton's beat.

Depto. de Hacienda - Treasury Department

Diablo - It means devil but can be used like cool or OMG.

Diantre! - an expression of excitement, like wow.

Dolorosa - Literally, the painful. An alternative way to ask for la cuenta, or the check.

Dron - Garbage can. Likely an Anglicism of drum.

E.

¡Ea rayo! - An expression of astonishment, roughly equivalent to Oh, shoot! in American English.

¡Ea' Diantre!- Puerto Rican slang for Oh, my God! Wow!.

Embuste - A lie.

¡Es mas puta que las gallinas! - Literally to be more promiscuous than chickens. As slang, very active sexually, slutty.

¡Esa es una píldora! - A compliment, like the English phrase You're a beast!

¡Esnu! - You're nude, naked!

¡Está brutal! - Literally, that's brutal. As slang, it's either a compliment or an insult, depending on context.

¡Está pasao! - Literally, It's the most fun, or the greatest thing, awesome. Used colloquially to tell someone they have crossed the line by doing something inappropriate.

¡Está que estilla!- This phrase can be used to describe a fine-looking person, or to describe someone who is furious.

¡Estás bueno/a! - You're hot!

Estas del carajo - You're too much. You're some piece of work.

You're way out of line.

¡Estás tenso, papá! - Literally, You're tense, daddy! A satirical phrase referring to homosexuality popularized by actor and comedian Sunshine Logroño.

¡Estás tripeando en ketchup! - You're in a natural high, without the use of any substance.

¡Estás tripeando! - Literally, you're tripping! Said when someone is high, or when someone's opinion on an issue is askew.

Echa caldo - Literally means that to give broth. Spoken when something is cool.

Echa pa' ca - Come over here. It is used to call someone over to you.

Echar leña al fuego - Literally, to add wood to the fire. As slang, to add to a controversy.

Echar un polvo - Literally, to throw dust, alluding to the biblical passage, Ashes to ashes, dust to dust. As slang, to have sex and ejaculate all over your sex partner.

ELA - The Commonwealth, the Government.

Empache - That uncomfortable, overstuffed feeling from over eatingfood on Thanksgiving.

Empalagoso - 1. Food flavored, too sweet, too heavy, or too cloying that give one un empache. 2. Someone who is extremely gentle.

En el carro de Don Fernando, un ratito a pie y otro andando - Literally, translates to Mr. Fernando's car, sometimes on foot and the rest of the time walking. So, in other words, when afoot.

En el jurutungo viejo - Somewhere far, far away, and hard or tiresome to get to, like Timbuktu.

En el mundo de la Farandula – Literally, in celebrity land or having to do with Actors/Actresses, Theatre, and the like.

En la falda del piloto - Literally, in the airplane pilot's lap. As slang it means being screwed.

En lo que el hacha va y viene, el palo descansa. - A rest period between bad situations. The lull before the storm.

En lo que el palo va y viene – While you are at it . . .

Eñagotar - To kneel down.

Enchismao - Contraction of ensimismado. Someone who is peeved.

Encojonao/a - Contraction of encojoinado from cojones. Your gonads glow red in anger. Pissed off.

Enñagotar –To kneel.

Entrega'o - A hardcore person.

Escante - To make heat, as in have sex.

Ese - A homeboy or homie.

Ése salió por lana y llegó trasquilao - Literally, This one left for wool and arrived sheared. As slang, a person headed out for something and came back worse than when he left.

Esmallao - Contraction of desmadayado. Meaning to feel faint. To be really hungry.

Esmandao - Contraction of desmandado. Going very fast, going too fast.

Esmonguillao - Contraction of esmonguillad, flabby. Somebody in a weakened condition or something that is way softer than usual.

Esos son otros veinte pesos - Meaning, that is an entirely different subject.

Está como refajo de loca - Someone whom is very drunk.

Está de película - Literally, It is from the movies. Used when something is finished, or when someone acts, like in a scene from a movie. Usually used when something awesome occurs.

Está más perdido que el hijo de Lindberg – Literally, He is more lost than Lindberg's (kidnapped) baby. As slang, someone lost forever.

Está más perdido que un juey bizco - Literally, You're more lost than a cross-eyed crab. It usually refers to someone confused and/or lost.

Está que estilla - It's cool.

Está quemao - Universal Spanish for he's or she is burnt up, in hot water, has done something wrong and was found out. Also, the dried-out feeling in the mouth after a long night's drinking.

Estar pela'o - To be broke.

Estar por la luna - Literally, to be on the moon. To be clueless.

Estas mas perdido que Rolandito - Literally, You are more lost than Rolandito, alluding to a child still missing since the early '90s.

Estinche– Anglicism for sting.

Estirar la pata - Literally, To stretch the leg. As slang, it means to die.

Ete pa'l carajo - Go to hell!

F.

Fajao - Contraction of fajado, derived from fajar, meaning to make a grand effort, as when working enough to work up break a sweat.

Falfullero - A show-off.

Faranduleando - Gossiping about celebrities.

Farandulera - A woman who likes dressing up for an event, any event, even when it means going to her front porch or dressing up like a movie star.

Farandulero - A groupie, a fan who faithfully follows their favourite artist or TV show.

Farfullero - Derived from farfullar, to mumble. A mumbler, a show-off, always speaking nonsense.

Fiao - Contraction of fiado. From fiar, to lend out, to loan.

Fiebrú - Someone who is feverish about fashion or cars. An aficionado, an enthusiast.

Filotiao - Derived from the slang word filoteado, which is further derived from the word filete, which means a steak filet. As slang, to be dressed very sharply and all your clothes neatly ironed.

¡Fo! - Gross, nasty or disgusting. Derived from the English exclamation Faugh, voiced to express disgust.

Fófalo - A small pillow for babies or a small pillow for stress relief when squeezed.

Fofo - Bland, lacking substance and referring to bland food or someone weak.

Fostro – 1. Spanglish for the venerable dance known as the Foxtrot. 2. A bad, uncomfortable situation you want out of.

Franfura - The venerable hot dog.

Fresa – In textbook Spanish, una fresa is quite literally the noble strawberry. But in Puerto Rico, as slang, it is a very silly, superficial, childlike girl or woman who enjoys pop music. This slang word can be either an insult or a backhanded compliment. When used as an insult, it means the person is immature and silly. As a compliment, it means the person is innocent, naive, and childlike.

Frikitona - From the Spanish word coqueta, but can mean a freak in bed.

Friquear - To freak out.

Fronte - Attitude. The phrase, Tener fronte, means having an attitude or putting up a false front.

Fuetazo - To whip a horse. To spank or to punish a girl.

G.

Gafas - Sunglasses.

Galán - Standard Spanish for a beau. Someone who looks elegant or dandy. It also means the lead actor.

Ganso - A wiseguy.

Gas pela - Literally gas peels, but can mean showing heat from a woman, as in body heat.

Gasolina - Literally gas, but it can mean heat as well.

Gata/Gato - Hot chicks or hot guys.

Gavette or Gabete - Literally, the shoelace. As slang, a loose woman (Like as loose as a shoelace), a slut or promiscuous woman.

Germ - A street term used to denigrate Puerto Rican people with light coloured skin. Short for German this term is derogatory.

Girla - Refers to women.

Gistro - A G-string or thong.

Gomas - Tires.

Grifo(a)- A light-skinned, light-haired, black person.

Guagua - Any large motor vehicle such as an SUV, a city bus or a full-size pick-up truck.

Guares - Twins.

Guatapanazo - A hard punch inflicted on someone or oneself.

Guayar - Literally to grind. As slang, dancing doggy-style.

Güebón - Big-balled (testicled) meaning a complete and total asshole.

Gufear -To goof around or to joke around.

Gufiao - Contraction of gufeado, an anglicism for goofy. Cool, or awesome.

Guillao or Guille – Prideful, or pride. The phrases Estar guillao and Tener guille mean to have a big ego, to be prideful, or being full of oneself.

Guineo - Banana.

Guingambó - The mallow flowering plant Okra, also known as ladies' fingers, bhindi, bamia, ochro, or gumbo.

Gusarapo - Literally, a tadpole. But it also refers to the larval stage of mosquitoes or sea monkeys. Renacuajo, however, is the correct Spanish word for this slang.

H.

Hacer brusca - Literally, to make tough. To skip class. To play hooky.

Hacer de tripas corazones – Literally, To make hearts out of guts. As slang, to make something good out of a bad situation.

Hacerse el loco - Literally, to pass off as crazy. To try ignoring or distance oneself from a situation as if it had never happened.

Hangear - To hang out with someone. In textbook Spanish: Pasar tiempo con alguien.

Hartarse de mamey - To take advantage of benefits.

Hijo 'e puta - Literally, son of a bitch, a contraction of Hijo de puta. As slang, a daring person.

Hijo de culebra no nace redondo – Literally, the son of a snake is not born round. Refers to someone who is like their parents. Alluding to the proverbial axiom that an acorn does not fall far from the tree.

Hijo de gato caza raton - Literally, the son of a cat will hunt rats. As slang, it is a synonym for the Nature of the beast.

Hijo de la gran puta - A big, son of a bitch.

Hijo e puta - Refers to a daring person or the son of a whore or bitch.

Hijo/hija del lechero - Literally, the son/daughter of the milkman. As slang, it describes a child who might not look much like his parents or lighter or darker-skinned than his siblings. Old school joke that a child might have been conceived from infidelity.

Horita (also spelled Orita) - Later on, but not right now. Not to be confused with Ahorita, used in most of Latin America, which means right now.

Hostia - Que hostia! A curse expressing extreme anger and hate. In Old Spanish, hostia is the body of Christ in the Catholic Church.

Huelebicho - Literally, a cock sniffer. A pejorative adjective for an insufferable person.

Huevon - Refers to a lazy person, or someone with giant testicles.

Huevos – Literally, eggs. As slang, testicles.

Huirle como el diablo a la cruz - Literally, to run from it as the devil runs from the cross. As slang, to forcefully avoid something.

I.

Iguaca - A rare species of endangered parrot typically found in El Yunque National Forest, located Northwest of San Juan.

Incordio - Someone who behaves annoyingly.

Insecto - Literally, an insect. As slang, a traitor.

Ir a to'a – To do something at any cost.

Ir pa chirola - Literally, to go to jail. To be incarcerated.

Irse pa' la isla - Literally, to go to the island. To leave the San Juan metropolitan area and travel to towns elsewhere on the island. To go out into the countryside of Puerto Rico.

J.

Jaiva – 1. Vagina or cunt. 2. Smart business person.

Jalao como timbre de guagua – Pulled out (as taut) as a bus bell. Someone thin.

Jalcoal - Anglicism slang for hardcore, used by teens to describe something extreme.

Jaleo - Standard Spanish word for a cheerful ambiance. As slang, to be nauseated, dizzy.

Jamaquiar - Derived from the Taino word hamaca, from which the English word hammock derives. Jamaquear means to grab somebody and manhandle them.

Jamona - Literally, a ham. As slang, used to describe a woman who has never married.

Jampiarse - Slang for Old Spanish Zamparse. To eat something whole. To eat to excess in an uncouth manner.

Janguear - To hang out.

Jangueo - A place to hang out or around.

Janguiar - Hanging out, to hang out.

Jara - A police vehicle.

Javao - A white man with a black man's physiognomy. On the mainland of the United States of America, they consider themselves black.

Jebo - An extremely attractive person of either sex. Also used for the person you are dating.

Jediondo - Foul-smelling, stinking (apestoso, hediondo).

Jevo - Boyfriend/girlfriend.

Jibarit Johnson (pronounced Yibarit) - A Puerto Rican who acts in a low-class manner. Ignorant and proud of it.

Jibaro - Someone from the countryside/mountainside of Puerto Rico, eg, a highlander, a hillbilly, or a peasant. It also refers to someone unaware of something all over the news, which is to say, someone, disconnected from the modern world.

Jicotea - A turtle.

Jienda - To get drunk.

Jincho - Someone very white or fair-skinned.

Jincho papujo - A person with very white or fair skin.

Jiribiya - An overactive child who will not sit still.

Jodienda - Derived from joder, to be screwing around. Something that bothers or annoys you.

Jodiendo la pita - A continuously annoying action by someone.

Messing around.

Jolgorio - Revelry. Lively and noisy festivities, especially where large amounts of alcohol are imbibed.

Jorobar - Euphemism for joder. To be bothersome.

Jorobeta - Something or somone annoying.

Josear/Joseador - Anglicism for hoser. To take advantage of something or someone or a situation.

Joya - A jewel, also used for a pond or swimming hole.

Joyete – Diminutive, for a little hole. Another word for butthole.

Joyo, Hoyo - A hole. Refers to the anus or butt crack.

Jugo de China - orange juice.

Jurutungo viejo - A borough in the town of Jayuya. Before cars and roads, it was a very inaccessible place. As slang, a distant place very far away and difficult to access.

Juyilanga - To leave or to abruptly leave.

Juyilanga coger la juyilanga - To be gone for a while.

Juyir - To flee (huir).

L.

Lambe queso - Hit in the back of the head, from the bottom up.

Lambeojo - Literally means eye licker, but refers to a brown noser or ass kisser.

Lambón - Brown-noser, lambe-ojo.

Las Quimbambas - Middle of nowhere. See Las Sinsoras, Jurutungo viejo.

Las Sínsoras - A far off place. Similar to El Jurutungo Viejo

Las ventas del carajo - Literally, in the periphery of hell. Used to express sheer dissatisfaction or anger towards someone.

Latejón - Describes a big thing.

¡La cagó! - He blew it!

Le dieron como a pandereta Aleluya o Pentecostal – Literally, They gave it to him like a tambourine at a Pentecostal church. As slang, describes when someone received a brutal beating.

Le supo a plato curtio - Literally meaning, it tasted like dirty dishes. As slang, they did not like the outcome of the situation.

Limbel - A frozen treat made from either natural fruits or sweet milk. Derived from the English surname: Lindberg, the famous pilot, the first man to fly across the Atlantic Ocean solo.

Limber - Also, limbel. A frozen treat made of natural fruits or sweet milk. Served on water-resistant paper, plastic or paper cup, or a Popsicle stick. Generally sold out of the homes and not in stores. The word originates from the last name of Charles Lindbergh, during his visit to the Island in 1928, when the islanders noticed how cold emotionally he was compared to the warmth of locals.

Lechón - Literally, a roast pig.

Lechóna - In the feminine form, the word describes a big, old car or a woman with an, especially broad fanny.

Limones - Small breasts.

Locón/locona - 1. Crazy. 2. An equivalent to dude, chick or buddy.

Lonchera – Lunchbox.

Lo tienes quemao - You've burned it out, as in You like something so much that you're burning it out, for example, by wearing the same clothes too often or even every day.

Longanisa - A debt paid in installments refers to the links in a long string of sausages.

M.

Maceta - 1. Literally, the mallet in a mortar. 2. A penis. 3. Also, cheapskate; someone who never contributes philanthropically.

Mafutera - Maf'u is slang for Marihuana, so naturally, it follows that mafutera is slang for a pothead or stoner.

Mahones - 1. Mahón, the capital of the Spanish Island of Minorca. 2. Blue jeans.

Mai - Derived from old Castilian, short for mami (which means and pronounced the same as mommy). A term of endearment for females.

Majadero - From the verb majar, to mash. A fool who persists in foolishness.

Maldita sea la madre que te pario - Damn the mother fucking bitch who gave birth to you.

Maldito/maldita - Damn.

Mamabicho - Cocksucker.

Mamalón - Derived from mamar, to suckle. 1. A large, dumb, clueless individual. 2. A mama's boy.

Mamao - 1. A cock sucker. 2. Also, a wimp.

Mamey - 1. Mammee fruit. 2. Easy stuff. Mameyes grow in tall trees. Accordingly, one has to wait for them to fall to the ground to harvest and enjoy them.

Mameyaso - A hard hit.

Mami - Mom, but usually refers to female friends, family, etc.

Mandulete - Standard Spanish for a lazy and annoying useless man, similar to Manganzón but applies to lethargic bums of all ages.

Manganzón - A full-grown man who behaves like a child and has to be looked after. The stereotypical man-child.

Mangao - Contraction of mangado, derived from the ancient Spanish verb, mangar, to catch a cheat or wrongdoer.

Mangar - From the Old Spanish Caló gypsy dialect, to catch someone doing something wrong or cheating.

Mango Bajito - As in low-hanging mango, Easy pickings, wussy, punk-ass, wuss,.

Mano! - The human hand, but also shortfor hermano/brother. An exclamation meaning: Hey, bro!

ManoBro - From the word hermano, meaning brother, a popular greeting between friends.

Maricón/Maricóna - Faggot, queer, or asshole.

Mariposa - Literally, a butterfly. As slang, an offensive slur for a gay man.

Marquesina - A house party.

Mas abajo pisó Colón - Literal translation: [Christopher] Columbus stepped lower than that. A complaint voiced when someone steps on your toes.

Más claro no canta un gallo - Literal translation: a rooster does not sing any clearer than this. As slang, it couldn't be any clearer or more explicitly stated.

Más fea que una mordia de un puerco – Literally, uglier than a pig's bite. The phrase describes a repulsive person.

Mas feo que Julito - Uglier than Little Julius, a very ugly man.

Mas larga(o) que la esperanza de un pobre - Longer than the hope of a poor man. Derived from hope that in the long run a situation will improve.

Más lento que un suero 'e brea - Slower than tar dripping.

Más lento que una caravana de cobos - Literal translation: Slower than a caravan of crabs. As slang, something or someone moving very, very slowly.

Más lento que una caravana de cojos - Slower than a traffic jam of cripples. Something or someone very slow-paced.

Más papista que el Papa – More Popist than the Pope himself, or more Christian than the Pope. Someone who, without being part of a situation, adamantly opines about it.

Más pelao que la rodilla de un cabro - Literally, to have less hair than a goat's knee. As slang, the hair stands for a lack of money to describe someone poor with no money at all.

Más perdido que un juey bizco – More lost than a cross-eyed land crab. As slang, someone who is poor or who has precious little money.

Mas trucos que la correa de Batman - More tricks, more gadgets than Batman's belt. As slang, a tricky person.

Mas viejo que el frio - Older than the cold, something or someone really old.

Masacote - Refers to a rather large penis.

Matando tiempo - Killing time.

Mazeta - Stingy

Me cago en tu mai (pai) - This vulgarism, sometimes voiced during traffic by taxi drivers, tthreatens defecating on someone's parents.

Me importa un bicho - Literally, to care for a dick. As slang, I don't give a rat's ass.

Me meo de la risa - So funny I wet my pants.

Me saca - Getting on your nerves, annoying. Essentially, me saca de quicio, shortened to: me saca.

Me tienes un lado seco - Voiced when someone is fed-up with a situation. You are driving up the walls/crazy.

Me tienes un ojo hinchado - Literally, I've got a swollen eye and used to express frustration when someone is fed up with a situation.

Me tienes una teta hinchada y la otra en proceso - Literally, You've made one of my tits inflamed, and the other is getting there. As slang, you're pissing me off!

Me tienes un huevo hinchado. - Literally, You've made one of my testicles inflamed. Used when someone is totally fed-up with a situation

Me voy a caballo y vengo a pie. - I left on a horse and came back on foot. An expression of dissatisfaction about a situation wherein you might invest maximum effort for very little in return. Or a situation where you were better off when you started than you ended.

Melaza - Molasses, which is nothing less than pure sugar cane juice. As slang it is used to say that something, someone, or a situation is excellent or sweet.

Melón – A melon, a sandia. It also refers to an Independentist (Green Party) who votes for the Popular Party (Red Party). A voter who gives the appearance of being green on the outside but is red on the inside.

Melones - Big breasts.

Mero, mero - Said to things that are 'off the hook'.

Metió la pata - Literally, he put his foot in it (his mouth). He made a mistake or blundered.

Mierda - Literally, shit.

Mijo - Contraction of Mi hijo (My son) but does not necessarily have to relate to your son or daughter.

Mimil - Baby talk for dormir, to sleep. Me voy a mimil. I'm going to sleep.

Mira –Look, look here.

.

Mi amigo el pintor! - Literally, my buddy the painter. Pokes fun at men who are unaware of being a cuckold. This phrase was popularized on a TV show called Desafiando a los Genios in which a naïve participant described his best friend, the painter, someone he believed was looking after his wife. When in reality, the wife was cheating with the painter.

¡Miércoles!- The day of the week, Wednesday, but also a euphemism for the word ¡Mierda! (Shit). Its English equivalent is Shoot! Voiced sounding like poised to say mierda, then transitioning in mid-word to miercoles.

Mira - Look.

Mira loco or Mira locón/locona - Look at this. Or, What's up, crazy!

Mira pescao – Literally, look here, you fish! As slang, spoken to express disapproval to someone for their actions, a way to back down someone trying to trick you.

Mistin - Miss Thing, from American black slang, popularized in the '80s by Guille, a character from the show Entrando Por La Cocina featured by actor Victor Alicea.

Molesta - Annoyed, mad.

Molleto or Moyeto - Literally, Old Spanish for a whole wheat/brown bread roll. As slang, an African American.

Mona Marti – Sarcastic name used to call someone an actor. As in, "You are being such a Mona Marti." Mona was a famous Puerto Rican (radio/TV/theater/movie) actress (1901–1985), who became for her role playing characters of mothers, grandmothers and, suffering or selfless nannies on Spanish TV soaps (Telenovelas).

Mondongo - Mondongo soup.

Mono - Literally, a monkey. As slang, cute. Said of a narcissist who thinks rather highly of himself.

Mono sabe palo que trepa y no trepa palo de limones - Literally, a monkey knows which tree to climb, conversely, not to climb lemon trees because they are copiously adorned with thorns. As slang, someone who rather wisely avoids picking on stronger adversaries.
.
Morcilla - Blood sausage.

Moreno/Morena - From the Old Spanish, Moro someone from North Africa, tawny skinned, dark-skinned, or black. A brunette.

Motín - A demonstration, usually against constituted authority. A riot.

Moyeto - Literally, Old Spanish for whole wheat, brown bread, a roll. Slang for a black person.

N.

Ná'- Contraction of Nada, meaning nothing.

Nalga - Buttocks.

Nebuloso - Cloudy, foggy, or vague. Both literal and figurative. As slang, untrustworthy.

Negrito/negrita - A term of endearment for any shade of Puerto Rican. It's related to the Puerto Rican versions of Baby or Honey as in your mate, which are Ay mi negra, Hola negro, Mira Negrita.

Nene / Nena - A boy. A girl. Commonly, used by adults to address small children, usually those who are related. As a term of endearment.

No inventes - Stop inventing, or don't make plans. Quit making things up.

No Je No Sé - I don't know.

¡No Jodas! - 1. Literally. Don't fuck with me! In Ancient Spanish the word Joder, came from Jodio, meaning a Jew. Because ancient Rome did not allow Christians to manage money and interest-bearing finances, Jews managed Banking and Savings, and Loans. Bankers loaned money at usurious monthly interests rates of 35%+. So naturally, it followed, una jodida equated with being screwed by the Jewish bankers. 2. Also used to say, no way!

¡No seas insecto! - Literally, Don't be an insect! Insecto is slang for a Narcotics Agent or a police informant. Normally pronounced with the last S in seas and the C in insecto muted for an accentuated slang.

No lo encuentran ni en los centros espiritistas - This phrase wryly describes someone so lost that they cannot even be found by a medium or by the spirits of the dead.

No perder ni pie ni pisada - Literally, to not miss the foot nor the step. To be constantly vigilant, especially as it refers to watching someone else's every move.

No te panikees - Do not panic.

No te rochees - Do not rush things, or don't worry.

Ñ.

Ñaqui - A small bite. A kiss or nip. From ñaca, a bite.

¡Ñoña es! - Literally, means shit, crap. As slang, it implies No way, eh?!

Ñoño - A whiny person. Also, a naive person who cannot stand up for himself/herself. See also añoñar.

O.

¿Oíte? - Did you hear?

Orejita - Literally, little ear. As slang, a tip, or a helpful hint.

Oricua - A native son or daughter of Borinquen, the island's original name.

Orita - Later on, not right now. Soon. Not to be confused with the similar-sounding word Ahorita, which in other Latin countries, means right now.

Otros 20 pesos – Literally, another $20.

Oso Blanco - Literally, the white bear. As slang, it means prison, referring to Río Piedras State Penitentiary, so nicknamed because the cement used to build it was imported from Venezuela and branded Oso Blanco (The White Bear).

P.

Pa' ca - Contraction of Para and aca, meaning: over here.

Pa' lla - A contraction of para alla, meaning: over there.

Pa'i - Old Spanish for Papa, Short for papi (daddy). Also, a term of endearment for males.

Pa'l - Contraction of Para el, which means for him.

Pa' lante - Contraction of Para adelante, move forward.

Pa'- Contraction of Para. Meaning for, as in to do something.

Pa'tras como el cangrejo - To fail to make headway or to refer to someone who will make no progress. Going backward, like a scuttling crab.

Pai - Old Spanish for Papa, the abbreviation for papi (daddy). Also, a term of endearment among men.

Paja - Masturbation.

Pajaro/pajarito - Literally, a bird or little bird. As slang, a penis, or little penis.

Palmolive - A green bottle of Heineken beer.

Palo - Literally, a tree. As a slang word, it means an alcoholic drink, usually a shot.

Pana - Breadfruit, Buddy, Pal.

Pana - In Puerto Rico, slang for breadfruit.

Panna or Pana- Buddy- breadfruit in Puerto Rico)

Papi - Dad. But usually refers to male friends and family.

Papisongo (male)o Mamisonga (female) - Sexual symbol.

Paquete - Literally, package. As slang, a lie.

Paquetero – Liar.

Pariguallo/a - A simpleton. A person from the country or someone uneducated.

Parkeado/a' - To be parked.

Parkear- Anglicism for parking a car. The correct term in Spanish is estacionar.

Parkiao - Parked. For comparison, estacionado is proper textbook Spanish.

Pasa'o - Too much, too ripe (fruit).

Pasar el Niagara en bicicleta – Literally, to cross Niagara Falls riding on a bicycle. As slang, to overcome great obstacles. Popularized by Juan Luis Guerra with El Niagara en bicicleta.

Pasteles - Boiled pies.

Pasto - An herb, either a common weed or marijuana.

Pataleta - When a spoiled little child repeatedly stomps the floor in anger or when an adult over-reacts or throws a hissy fit.

Pato(male)/pata(female) - Literally, a Duck. As slang, a fag or lesbian as in homosexual, or gay.

Pato/Pata - Literally, duck. As slang, a fag, or homosexual.

Patatús - Standard Spanish for a conniption fits. The non-specific ailment involves fainting or hot flashes that cause a commotion. Typically afflicts older Puerto Rican women in crowded places.

Pava - The traditional straw hat worn by Puerto Rican sugar cane harvest laborers, is used as the Partido Popular Democratico de Puerto Rico political party.

Pegandole cuernos - Giving him/her horns. Someone faithless or adulterous.

Pedir pon - To hitchhike.

Pela pa bajo - Take off clothes. Desvestirse, quitarse la ropa. - Undress, take your clothes off.

Pelado - Literally, peeled. As slang, it implies being penniless or broke.

Pelao como rodilla de cabra - Literally, bare like a goat's knee, as slang means broke or lacking money.

Pelar la yuca - To peel back the yuca, As slang, peeling back the foreskin in order to pleasure oneself.

Peldona 'sae - Sorry, eh?! An abbreviation for, Perdona, sabes? in grammatically-correct Spanish.

Pellisco de ñoco - A pinch from an amputee (ñoco). As slang, an impossibility, something that will never come to pass.

Pendejiando or Pendejeria –Clowning around or wasting time.

Pendejo/pendeja - A jerk, dumb, slow-witted, or someone who is easily taken advantage of.

Pensando en pajaritos preñao - Literally, musing about pregnant little birds. As a slang word, it describes someone with their head in the clouds daydreaming.

Peo - Contraction for pedo, a fart.

Perico - Coke (cocaine).

Perreo/Perrear - Describes how reggaeton is danced. As a noun or verb, the word means doggy-style sex, dancing closely together, or grinding.

Perro que huele carne – Literally, A dog that smells meat. As slang, it describes a situation where a person believes something he wants is within reach.

Peseta – A 25 cent piece from coinage used in Puerto Rico during Spanish colonial times.

Peste a chinchorí del monte- Very stinky.

Peste a Moscovito viejo - Stench of an old Muscovite, very stinky.

Phillie - A joint/cigarette.

Picao - Tipsy.

Pichear – 1. Literally, to pitch. Looking to get something from someone. 2. To ignore. 3. To ask someone to forget about something.

Pie en Polvorosa – Literally, to flee at full speed, raising a big cloud of dust. (polvorosa). To get away from somewhere in a big hurry.

Pinche - Darn, as in ¡Pinche pendejo! Darn asshole!

Pinga - A penis, dick, cock.

Pionono - Banana-beef fried cake.

Pipa - Belly.

Pipiolo - PIP party member

Pipón/a - Someone with a protruding belly or gut.

Piragua - 1. The Taino word for a canoe. 2. A treat made from hand-shaved ice doused with colored/flavored syrup and traditionally served in a paper cone. A snow cone.

Piragüero/piragüera - A piragua vendor. Also describes a player or someone who uses many pick-up lines.

Piropo - Sexually aggressive flattery as in catcalls.

Pisaicorre - A mini-bus.

Pista - A music track.

Pitorro - Moonshine rum.

Playero/a - A beach bum.

PNP – The New Progress Party.

Pollo - Literally, a chicken. As slang, though, it means a couple kissing in a pecking manner. Mwah!

Pompeaera - Pumped up.

Pon - A lift or ride in a vehicle. Dar pon - To give a lift.

Ponte en 4 - A sexual reference, meaning to get down on all fours, having sex doggy-style.

Por el techo – Literally, through the roof. As slang, someone who is very mad.

Por la maceta - A maceta is a mallet. As a slang word, it implies approval by mallet blow. Something that you approved of, like great, or good deal, or was awesome.

Por la puñeta – Literally, the fist. As slang, it refers to a place located far away.

Por un tubo y siete llaves - Through a tube and seven keys. Denotes an abundance, an oversupply, usually of food. At Thanksgiving or Christmas, a hostess will invite guests to take food home with them because "There's food here por un tubo y siete llave."

Hacerme la puñeta - Means masturbation, derived from the word puño, specifically male masturbation (fist).

Punto carajo - A place far away or inaccesible. Sometimes campo carajo.

Puta/puto - A whore, bitch, or slut. A whore, conjunction of prostituta. Or simply an asshole.

Puya - Coffee without any milk or sugar. Bitter Coffee. In Spanish, the word puya means the point of a lance.

Q.

¡Que fleje! - Fleje is a fling, a floozy. As a slang phrase, it implies, 'How ugly!

¡Que guasón eres! - A guasón is joker, a prankster. You are such a prankster!

¡Que peste a sicote! - Literally, what a bad feet smell! Sicote is standard Spanish parlance for bodily filth and grime mixed with sweat, especially the feet.

¡Que santo guatapanazo se metió! - Getting hit really hard.

¿Qepota? - Slang for Hello or What's up?

¿Qué es la qué estapajando?, ¿Qué es la qué hay? - What's up?

¿Qué pasa pai? - A contraction for ¿Qué pasa compai?, itself a contraction for ¿Qué pasa compadre? Meaning, What's up, dude?

Que fue?- What happened?

Que mal le va - When someone is doing something wrong, it means it is going bad for them, or when things are not going so well.

Que pao' (que paso) - As in Que pao' quien carajo tu eres? What happened? Who the fuck are you?

Que rico - Literally, it feels good, or it tastes good. Commonly voiced while having sex.

Que tronco 'e cancha - A cancha is a basketball court and tronco means a piece of. As slang, this figure of speech is an esoteric way of remarking how a girl has a big ass and associating said ass with a gathering place where young men are fond of congregating.

Quedar en la página de Cheo - Similar to the phrase, Quedar retratao. Based on an editorial feature of El Vocero, a Puerto Rican daily newspaper that strategically placed a cartoon named Cheo alongside the editorial and reader's section denouncing misbehavior or corruption of local politicians.

Quedar retratao - To clearly be guilty, having been being caught red-handed in the act, to be exposed.

Quemao - A hangover.

Quemar - Literally to burn, as slang refers to smoking marijuana.

Quenepa - The Quenepa fruit.

R.

Rasca yuca–Literally, to peel back the yuca. As slang, to peel back the foreskin in anticipation of sexual activity.

Raitrú - Something true or correct, used to show agreement.

Rajar(se) - Literally to split. This flexible verb can mean leaving a place, quitting a job, getting drunk, or wearing oneself out fornicating.

Rampleteando - Going out to party to find a sex partner in anticipation of a one-night stand.

Rampletera(ro) - A promiscuous person.

Ranquearse - To score cool points.

Rebellusca - Someone angry or in a foul mood.

Rebuleo or rebuliar - Conducting oneself with deportment like an experienced champion. This reference harkens back to the days when Michael Jordan was the MVP star of the NBA Chicago Bulls.

Relajar(se) - To relax, meaning to have fun, joke around or engage in wild behavior at a party.

Relajo - Din or racket. The phrase ¡Deja el relajo! Translates as Stop playing around. Similar in meaning to ¡Deja el gufeo!

Repeplé - When a real mess occurs.

Revulú or revolu - Derived from the word revuelto (messed-up or a disaster). Denotes a scandal, a loud commotion, or confusion.

Rola - To keep it moving.

Roncar - To snore. As slang, to bluff, to lie.

S.

Saca la yuca - Get the yuca out, an expression used to motivate someone to be at peace and put an end to anger.

Sal pa' fuera - Get out, or go outside. A commotion or melee erupts inside and spills over outside, causing the entire room to vacate.

Salió el tiro por la culata - The shot backfired. Describes when a plan backfires.

Salpafuera - a revolú or a real mess.

Sanamagan (pronounced with a seseo/lisp) - Bastard, derived from the son of a gun

Sandunguero - Party music. Related words: sandungueo, sandunguera, sandunguear, yakaleo, hangueo, baileteo, mamboteo, and zandungueo.

Sandwihe - Literally, a sandwich.

Sangano – Idiot. Describes someone acting stupidly or foolishly. A lazy man. Derived from the male bee (Zangano), whose sole duty in life to the beehive is to breed the queen.

Sanjuanero - Someone from San Juan.

Sapa - Literally, a female frog. As slang, a Hummer Army vehicle.

Saramanbiche (pronounced with a seseo/lisp) - Sumbitch.

Sata - A woman with a particularly strong sex drive.

Se alborota - To rampage insanely.

Se formó un corre y corre! - Confusion. Melee.

Se formó un sal pa fuera - A get-out-of-here-situation, or a violent situation from which many fled.

Se jodió la bicicleta - Literally, the bicycle got screwed. As slang, used to describe a situation that spiraled out of control, leaving no place to run.

Se lució el chayote - Chayote is a tasteless tropical fruit with a flavor only as good as its seasoning. Lucirse means to show off. This slang phrase is used to criticize a show-off.

Siéntate a esperar - Sit down and wait! Its English equivalent is: Don't hold your breath.

Sin Jockey - To be single, without a boyfriend, alone without a male escort.

Sin verguenza – Literally, to be without shame. A good for nothing, a bum.

Sínsoras - A distant place.

Sipi Dame un sipi- Literally and figuratively, let me sip your drink.

So anormal - You're so damned stupid/weird! Anormal is the Spanish word for abnormal, with a negative and insulting connotation.

Socio - Partner or friend.

Suelta como gabete - Literally, loose like a shoelace. It implies a female who will have sex with just about anyone.

T.

Taco - Literally, 1. A pool cue. 2. The heel of a shoe. 3. A Mexican snack. 4. As slang, it refers to an easy-going person.

Tante - To be full of. To show strong emotion.

Tanto nadar para ahogarse en la orilla! - So much swimming, only to drown at the shore. A lamentation describing someone who came very close to success, only to fail.

Tapón - Literally, a cork or a stopper. As slang: 1. A traffic jam. 2. A short-statured person.

Tarambana - A person of poor judgment. A good for nothing.

Tarantala - Something shady, suspicious, or bizarre.

Tato - Tato' hablao. - Contraction for Esta todo hablado. Meaning everything's cool. We have an understanding. Typically voiced at the end of a conversation before each person goes their own way.

Te cagaste del miedo - You pooped your pants in fear.

Te cogieron de mango bajito - Literally, they took you for a low mango (easy to pick). As slang, they took you for a fool. Used when someone was easily taken advantage of.

Te dan pon y quires guiar. - Literally, They give you a ride, but you want to drive. Used when you give a person a chance, and they fail.

Te dieron chino - Literally, they gave you Chinese. He humped your bump!

Te gua a dar un mamellazo - I'm going to hit you with a (big) mamey!

Te lo metieron bien mongo – Literally, they screwed you with a limp penis. The phrase is used to complain when someone took you for the fool.

Te pones una plancha de zinc en la cabeza y eres una letrina ambulante! - Literally, You place a zinc plank on your head, and you're a walking latrine.- As slang, you stink big time!

Tecato/a - 1. A drug addict, a junkie who uses drugs intravenously. 2. An inferior copy, a counterfeit of poor quality. Derived from manteca (lard) or heroin that tecatos inject into their veins.

Tener complejo de alguien - To have a delusion of being like someone else by adopting certain characteristics of that person.

Teta -1. Tit, breast (mammary gland). 2. The end slice of French bread.

TeVeGuia - TV Guide.

Tiene mazamorra en los dientes - Mazamorra is the ancient Spanish word for blancmange. Translation, "He has blancmange/egg custard stuck in his teeth." An embarassment.

Tirar - To throw, or to throw away, can also mean to hit on a person, to make a pass.

Tú eres bien fiebrú/fiebrua - Derived from the word fever. A compliment used when admiring someone's passion, particularly cars or car racing.

Tú sí que eres presentado. Tú eres bien presentado, or So presentado. - To present yourself uninvited, meaning, you're very nosy, forcing your presence here. Stop being nosy!

Tienes yuca conmigo - Literally, You have a yuca with me. As slang intimates, someone bearing a grudge against you.

Tipeja - Standard Spanish for a twerp of a woman. Slang for a nonexistent girlfriend created in the mind of a very jealous woman.

Tipo - Literally, type. Standard Spanish for fellow. Use it when you cannot remember someone's name. That guy, what's his name . . . It can also be used for someone whose real name you don't want to say aloud, in which case, it would have a derogatory connotation.

Tipo raro - A weirdo.

Tirar (Te tiraste a alguien) - To make out with someone who isn't your boyfriend or girlfriend.

Tirar la pata - Contraction of Estirar la pata. Literally, to stiffen your leg. As slang, to kick the bucket, to die.

.

Tirar-Tirar - Literally to throw. As slang, to hit on someone.

Tití - Auntie

To'a - Contraction of Toda, as in all.

Tomar el pelo - To take someone's hair. As slang, meaning to take someone for a fool, to fool someone, pulling one's leg.

Toque - Literally, touch. To take a hit of an illegal substance.

Toribio - Toribio is derived from toro (bull) and thus implies being tagged by the horns of infidelity. Toribio was the name of a TV character who was a cuckold and has come to mean a cuckold in general.

Tosta'o - Nuts, crazy.

Toto tota, totito - 1. Vulva, vagina, crotch, pudenda. A reference to female genitalia when speaking to young girls. 2. Somone who is a pussy.

Tra - Meaning from behind (de tras), or a contraction of traga to swallow (semen). Often used in reggaeton, it can be used perrer (doggy-style) a woman.

Tráfala - Describes a person not brought up well, with poor manners, and who dresses trashy. Riff-raff, a ghetto person.

Trigueño - Bronzed, medium-dark skin, suntanned.

Tripear - To move up. To trip, as in tripping, to act foolish or say things that are not true.

Truckiar - To kiss or to make out with someone you just met.

Tu tío corre bicicleta sin sillín - Literally, your uncle rides a bike without the seat, as in with a stick up his anus, implying your uncle is a sodomite.

Tumbacoco - An obnoxiously loud vehicle fitted with a loud sound system. 1. Refers to knocking down coconuts with noise. 2. Doing damage to the political party, symbolized by the coconut palm.

Tumbar - Literally, to knockdown. As slang, to steal something.

U.

¡Uepa! - Cool!

¡Uva! - Literally, a grape. Often used when good news is received.

V.

Vela Güira- An opportunistic man or woman who preys on someone else's romantic partner or a basketball player who just wants to score easy layups.

Vellón - A nickel. The word vellón derives from the French billon.

¡Vete pa'l carajo! - Go to hell!

¡Vete pa'l Caribe Hilton! - The Puerto Rican version of ¡Vete al carajo!, meaning Go to hell! or Fuck you! or fuck off! Point of reference, The Caribe Hilton is a hotel in the San Juan area.

Vete pa la carcel - To go to jail.

Viejo verde - Literally, green, old man. As slang, a horny, dirty old man.

¿Viste? - An exclamation for, See?! Did you see it? Used to challenge or to prove someone wrong.

¿Vite? - Did you see it?

Vive en el carajo – Literally, you live far away. As slang, You are out of touch with reality.

Viviendo del mamey - Living the life of Riley on welfare, public employment, or an easy job.

¡Volando bajito! - Literally, flying low. As slang, it describes speeding drivers or people who try to commit a given act without getting caught.

W.

Watermelon - While watermelon is referred to as Sandia in most Spanish-speaking countries, in Puerto Rican slang, the word describes a fine-looking person or someone furiously angry.

¡Wepa! - Yelled loudly is an informal Puerto Rican greeting, like Hey! or Wow! Expressing surprise. Sometimes pronounced ¡Jepa! The slang word means: All right! Good job! Congratulations! Yeah! When saying, Wepa!, hold the letter-E for the longest amount of time and the letter-A for just as long.

Y.

Ya tu sabes - A common phrase meaning, You already know.

Yal/Yale - Women, girl, chick, broad.

Yerba mala nunca muere - The old axiom, "Bad weeds never die." equates with the American sayings, "Only the good die young," and "Bad blood never runs dry."

Yerba - Literally herb. As slang, Marijuana.

Yo sé como bate el cobre – Literally, I know how to beat the copper. As slang, I know what's going on here. Asserted in rebuttal to being told a lie.

¿Y qué? - Literally, "And what!? So what? Or, So what's up?

Yuca - Cassava, or yucca root. When used as slang, it means jerk, dork, or penis.

Yunque - Literally, a blacksmith's anvil. El Yunque is also a park Northwest of San Juan, reputed to have been visited by UFOs.

Z.

Zafacón - A trash can. Some sources assert it comes from the English word safety can. Others disagree because the word zafacón is also used in the Dominican Republic.

Zafaito - Out of place. Inappropriate, spoken when somebody has been disrespectful.

Zahir - An obsession.

Zángano - From the the male bee, the Zangano, whose sole duty to the beehive is to breed with the queen. As a slang word, it denotes a worthless idiot, either a female or male, who is stupid or foolish.

Zarrapastroso - A ragamuffin, a tramp.

Axioms

A.

A juyir, Crispín - Let's flee. Crispin. Slang for, We gotta get out of this place (if it's the last thing we ever do).

A las millas de chaflán - Driving too fast, speeding past someone, walking fast, or at high speed Used as a criticism. Chaflán means chamfer in English, as in the chamfered street corners of Barcelona, Spain, and Ponce, Puerto Rico. Denotes something done rapidly, alluding to the fact that a driver does not have to slow down as much transiting a chamfered street corner as a square corner.

A ti te daban con la correa de Batman - To imply that your parents physically abused you.

A ver si el gas pela - Literally, Let's see if the gas peels. As slang, let's see what happens when push comes to shove.

Arroz, que carne hay - Literally, Where's the rice to go with all that meat! As slang, having one thing and soliciting something else to complement it.

Así es el mambo - That's how to dance the mambo. As a slang phrase: that's the nature of the beast. That's how it is. What is, is.

Así es la cosa - It is what it is, like it or not.

C.

Chúpate esa en lo que te mondan la otra(like an orange) - Literally, sucking on a fruit, all the while ready for the next one. As slang, used when someone is being disciplined (usually your sibling) to express scorning and approval for some punishment given or some unexpected result occurs, such as a minor accident that results in minor pain or discomfort.

Como alma que lleva el diablo - Literally, as if the devil possessed their soul. As slang, to describe someone who left in a big hurry or very angry.

E.

En el carro de Don Fernando, un ratito a pie y otro andando -, Mr. Fernando's car, some of the time afoot and the rest of the time walking. Voiced when no car is available. A man without a horse is afoot.

En lo que el hacha va y viene, el palo descansa - A break between bad situations.

Enfiebrao Ahora todo el mundo esta enfiebrao con Justin Bieber. - Now everyone has Justin Bieber fever.

Ése salió por lana y llegó trasquilao - Literally, This one left for wool and came back sheared. Meaning a person went for something and came back worse than when he left.

Está como refajo de loca - Refajo is an old ladies' undergarment. Literally, an unstable woman who would show what's under her skirt. Meaning someone very drunk.

Está como uva - Literally, like a grape. Someone slumbering in a deep sleep.

Esto es oro de la Palestina - Literally, this is gold from Palestine, meaning something of high quality, hard to find, or the best thing available on the market.

Esto es oro del que cago el moro - Literally, the gold that the Moor crapped in Mediaeval Spain. Back in the day, only Jews

81

and Muslims dealt in jewelry. So inexperienced Christians fell easy prey to unscrupulous non-Christian traders. The expression implies fake jewelry that merely looks like gold.

Estoy pidiendo cacao - Literally, I'm asking for cocoa. Voiced when hurt, drunk, or very tired after partying all night long. Almost like asking for forgiveness. Begging.

H.

Hablas cuando las gallinas mean - Literally, when hens pee. Used to tell someone to keep quiet, or else.

Hay que ver como se bate el cobre - To see how the copper is hammered, meaning to see how things turn out.

L.

La piña está agria - The pineapple is sour, meaning times are tough or no money or resources.

La última coca-cola de el desierto - Literally means The last Coca-Cola available in the desert. As slang, this phrase refers to an arrogant person who thinks of himself as indispensable, more so than he actually is.

Las cosas se pusieron a chavito prieto – Literally, things became a tight penny. Times are hard.

Las cosas se pusieron color de hormiga brava - Things have become the color of a fire ant. Describing a tough situation.

Las ventas del carajo - In the periphery of hell. Used to express sheer dissatisfaction with someone.

Le dieron como a pandereta de Pentecostal - They gave it to him like a tambourine at a Pentecostal church. Describes someone who endured a hard beating. They beat him like a drum.

Le supo a plato curtído - Literally, It tasted like dirty dishes. As slang, he did not like the outcome of a particular situation.

Lo tienes quemao -You've burned it out, as in You like something so much that you're burning it out by wearing the same clothes too often, or even every day.

84

Los huevos se pusieron a peseta - Eggs are worth a quarter each. Times are hard.

Los huevos se pusieron duros - The eggs have turned hard. Times are hard.

M.

Mira me dijeron que estabas enfermo. - Look, they told me you
were sick.

N.

No es fácil catchar sin careta - Life is not easy.

No es fácil catchar sin careta - Literally, it ain't easy to play catcher without a mask. Life is hard.

No es fácil quitarle el cuchillo a Rambo, pero se puede - It is not easy taking (John) Rambo's knife away from him, but it can be done. Inspired by author David Morrell's novel and Hollywood feature film: First Blood.

Q.

Quien a buen árbol se arrima, buena sombra lo cobija - An Old Spanish proverb literally offers, "He who takes shelter under a good tree gets the best shade."

Meaning one would benefit from being close to someone who is in a position to give you what you want or need. So naturally, it follows that if you want to succeed, you would be wise to get close to successful people. Conversely, if you hang around losers, you'll end up a loser. You are who your friends are.

Que tronco' e cancha or que tronco 'e batea - An esoteric way of saying that a girl has a big ass and associating it with a large gathering place that boys are fond of and like to frequent. A cancha is a basketball court, and tronco means a piece of a tree trunk.

S.

Se la/lo chupo la bruja - Literally, Got sucked by the Witch. He or she got caught without a way out of a sad, sad situation.

Se pusieron los huevos a peseta - Literally, an egg is now worth a quarter. Things got really bad. Times are hard all over.

Si eres mudo revientas - Literally, if you were mute, you would explode. Someone is bursting at the seams to speak their mind.

Un muerto hablando de un ahorcado - Literally, a dead man talking about a hanged man. Used to call attention to someone criticizing another person who ironically is in an identical predicament. In English, a pot calling the kettle black.

V.

Voy con mi corrillo al cine - Literally and figuratively, I'm going to the movie theater with my family (crew).

Y.

Y se le(s) está haciendo tarde - Literally, And it's becoming too late already! Or, you're running out of time! A sports phrase describing the situation when an individual or team is behind on scoring as the event nears its conclusion. The clock is ticking . . .

Words and Phrases

Basic Communication

Hola – Hello

Sí - yes

No - no

Gracias - Thank you (colloquially pronounced: gracia)

Buenos Dias - Good Morning

Buen Dia - Good Morning (more colloquial)

Buenos Tardes - Good Night

¿Como se dice? - How do you say?

¿Cómo está Ud? - How are you?

¿Cuánto es? / - How much is it?

¿Cuánto cuesta? - How much does it cost?

Habla inglés? - Do you speak English?

¿..... frances? -Do you speak French?

¿.....alemán? Do you speak German?

Por favor - please

No comprendo, - I don't understand this thing, ths fact)

No se entiendo I don't understand what you are saying.

Hable lento, por favor - Please speak more slowly

Lo siento - I'm sorry

No lo sé - I don't know

Aqui está - Here it is

¿Cómo se dice right en espanol? - How do you say right in Spanish?

¿Cómo se dice bonita en engles? - How do you say pretty in English?

izquierda – left

la derecha – right

rincon - corner, street corner.

Estoy buscando solamente, gracias - I am only looking, thank you.

¿Qué hora es? - What time is it?

esta mañana - this morning

esta tarde - this afternoon

esta noche - tonight

de ida y vuelta – roundtrip

casa de cambio - exchange house (for currency.)

Getting Around Town

¿Qué calle es esta? What street is this?

Cuán lejos queda? - How far is...

Aeropuerto - airport

Baños – toilet, bathroom

calle - street

plaza - square

mapa de carreteras - road map

¿Dónde esta? - Where is it?

pare - stop. On a bus, called out to request the bus driver stop.

puedo usar su telefono? - may I use your telephone?

Estoy perdido - I'm lost

La playa - the beach

el mar - the sea, ocean

¡Ayuda! /¡ Auxilio! - Help!

¡Ladrón! - Help! Thief!

¡Llame a la policia! - call the police

¡Llame a un médico! - call a doctor

¡Peligro! - Danger!!

En el restaurante/At the restaurant

Quiero pedir / Quiero ordenar - I'd like to order:
Mi amigo quisiera ordenar - my friend would like to order:
Deme la cuenta, por favor - Check please
caro - expensive
barato - cheap
tenedor - fork
cuchara, cucharita - spoon, teaspoon
taza - cup
cuchilla - knife
platos – plates
a la brasa/a la parilla - charcoal grilled
cocido – cooked
poco concido - rare
termino medio – medium
bien cocido - well done
desayuno - breakfast
almuerzo - lunch
la cena – dinner

Food

arroz - rice
azucar - sugar
bacalao - cod
calamares - squid
camarones - shrimp
cangrejo or juey - crab
carne - meat
cerdo - pork
coco - coconut
filete, bistec - steak
flan - caramel custard
franfura – frankfurter
fruta - fruit
guayabas - guavas
huevos - eggs
jamon – ham
Jugo de China - orange juice
langosta - lobster
lechon asado - roast pork
mangos - mangoes
mantequilla - butter

mofongo - Mashed plantain, broth, garlic and olive oil combined with meat or seafood.

pan - bread
pescado - fish
pimienta - black pepper
plátanos - bananas, plantains
platanos maduros - sweet plantains

pollo - chicken
postre - dessert
queso - cheese
sal - salt
salchicha - sausage
tocineta - bacon
verduras – vegetables

Counting

uno - one
dos - two
tres - three
cuatro - four
cinco - five
seis - six
siete - seven
ocho - eight
nueve - nine
diez - ten
once - eleven
doce - twelve
trece - thirteen
catorce - fourteen

quince - fifteen
diesiseis - sixteen
diesisiete - seventeen
diesiocho - eighteen
diesinueve - nineteen
veinte - twenty
treinta-thirty
cuarenta - forty
cinquenta-fifty
sesenta - sixty
setenta - seventy
ochenta - eighty
noventa – ninety
cien(to) - one hundred